Medlars

Geraldine Clarkson

Medlars

Shearsman Books

First published in the United Kingdom in 2023 by
Shearsman Books Ltd
PO Box 4239
Swindon
SN3 9FN

Shearsman Books Ltd Registered Office
30–31 St. James Place, Mangotsfield, Bristol BS16 9JB
(this address not for correspondence)

www.shearsman.com

ISBN 978-1-84861-868-8

ACKNOWLEDGEMENTS
Thanks to the editors of the following journals and presses, who first
published some of the poems included here: *Anthropocene, Beyond Words,
Blackbox Manifold, Butcher's Dog, The Dark Horse, Envoi, Festschrift for Tony
Frazer*, Grist Press (*We're All in it Together: Poems for a DisUnited Kingdom*,
ed. Michael Stewart, Stephen Ely & Kayleigh Campbell, Huddersfield
University, 2022), *Gutter Magazine*, Ice Floe Press, *The Interpreter's House,
Iota, Journal of Civic Architecture*, Live Canon, *Magma, New Boots and
Pantisocracies, Poetry Birmingham Literary Journal, Poetry London, Poetry
News, The Poetry Review, Shearsman* magazine & Shearsman Books,
smith | doorstop, *Tears in the Fence,* and Verve Poetry Press.

AUTHOR'S NOTE
A 'marplot' (see p. 86) is a meddlesome, interfering person.

Contents

So, in the strange retorts of medlars and sorb-apples
The distilled essence of hell.
The exquisite odour of leave-taking.

—D.H. Lawrence, 'Medlars and Sorb-Apples'

[A] gentle heart was broken. Whose? No one's
It's a figure like a frame among
medlars & briars…

—Alice Notley, 'Congratulating Wedge'

Everything you told me came untrue,

as if your eye at the witching hour
when you told us bedtime stories
was faulty on its target. Perhaps

your seer's hands, smooth
and oiled from washing up, slipped
in their tracing of force lines
on your crystal ball. Maybe

your too-hasty breath
flustered the tea leaves, dis-
torted picture portents
dredged on china.

Your prophecy that I might die
young faded
after you'd aired it eighteen times,
once each birthday, for bad luck.

The blade of your sibyl's claim
that I wasn't meant for marriage,
that lovers would recoil,
blunted (though I grasped it still).

And the old domestic curse –
that I would never write,
that words would fail to join –
the black source like treacle, stuck,

trickles freer with each poem that comes,
Mother.

Medlars

England like a medlar, unbletted.
When they come to score the cardboardy
hide, to get at the lush nostalgic mud
inside, the sting
causes them to backtrack
and search for better butter elsewhere.

Let the hard-to-grow fruit grow ruddy
like fat peasant cheeks
etched into blue glass sky,
not splayed on racy dishes for royalty –
the Kingdom split, grinning wide
at the hinges, creaking, just holding for now.

Apocalypse (Synopsis)

A thousand starlings plop like gobs of tar
from corned-beef skies, for no apparent cause.
Then fish, with twisted fins, and six-inch scars,
turn up in private gardens and offshore.
Domestic pets climb rooftops late at night
and yowl, as if, despite themselves, they felt
the pull of iron in their bloody bite –
a rankle or an itch below the pelt.
Grand beasts, like tigers, amble with their cubs
to play with ducklings fledging in the park;
soft-sheathe their claws behind the flower tubs;
excel at karaoke after dark.
Two-headed babies grizzle at the breast.
And tabloid hacks keep *schtum* – 'it's for the best'.

Myself as Medieval Horsewoman

after *Two Scenes from Der Busant (The Buzzard)*,
Tapestry, 1480–90, The Metropolitan Museum of Art

My medieval streak to the fore, blond horses
and my buzzard, a tarnished tame-ish bird behind
me, who am two-dimensional with a downturned mouth,
my opulent brocade slightly unlaced, and
a saddlebag – for my books, medlars, and picnic sweetbreads –
flung over jewelled harness straps. Our horses stepping
over bracken and oak-leaves mysteriously rising
from forest earth, innocent. And you, my companion
all gold-bestial in shaggy lion suit, on all fours, what are you
like. My horse, round-eyed, spiritual, prancing. Orchids climbing
decisively, derisively, around our borders. My arse
sliding down my horse-side. Mini-mountain
clouds. In a flat world, I clip my sighs.
A heavy crown I'd hardly noticed, deep-
sapphired. My uncertain glance, horseheadwards.
Rich rhenish braids, my bonds. Arrested as I dismount.
A banner over my head I cannot read.

Sidewinder

St John lost this prize-winning volume – *The Blue Fairy Book*, inscribed by his father. No music late at night from the Ark.

****

Book One
Mallory and Malachy breed for Egypt, seeking to populate pain. A mass of till, a chance moraine, brings a maroon quiet to the helm at dawn, a muted swoon. Lot looks out at last over a salty waste, his wife's waist encrusted in memory, the round of it. Copper céilí drums kettle in at the corner, all music pickled for the time.

Book Two
I would like – the captain's wife began – her voice querulous, unruly, like whalers or pirates were trying to rein it in with harpoons, but it soared to land in an ashram, found a home in a chantress's breast. Carry-on in the choir. Six exultant postulants pooled the evidence they'd pulled, ova and ova. But dark whistles and they can scarcely raise the purser. *You wonderful electric being*, the live-in widow coos to her landing lamp, lost in St Dominic and white.

Book Three
No-er, no-er, mock the twins, twirling fake handlebar moustaches over the rails, a little off. Doves squabble with olive boughs and boysen-berries.

Methuselah rejuvenates sappy knees with aloe.

****

The rain starts up again, rats return. Michael Archangel loiters near the figurehead, stands ready. All the quiet earth bends its ear.

Blaue Blaue Blaue

You have this, Mother: we are private here in our alcove, fresh-flowered each Friday; bowed to by devout schoolgirls, albeit perfunctorily...
[Albertine Alba's daughter (private correspondence)]

Blaue! Blaue! Blaue! And blaue your mantle, which is magnificent, and will keep us from ham.

We eat green leaves gathered from the herbarium Tue–Sat, in order to be less undeserving.

I composed something outstanding while I was waiting in the shower for the steam to clear and the blood to flow less fancily.

Machines all over town nudge pound coins into gutters and drains, enriching the rats who spend, spend, spend in unsecured kitchens – two preening like ladies-in-waiting on the sugar shelf.

Nallybance and the Light Potion

When Nallybance came among us, his sowed light – just a pinch at first into broken-cupped hearts which winced with the tart unexpectedness of it – was welcome. We lined up on the second day, Nallybance's lieutenant having telegraphed instructions. Two spoonfuls for the sickly kids – straight to the front of the queue. Lumpy ladies with pendulous bellies had theirs watered down, and just a single chaste spoon. Not many men were called. There were a few stripling boys with angel faces and bright less-than-beards who skipped in and took full draughts in clean ringing vessels. The girls mainly resisted, and by the end of the seventh day he had left us.

Dumpland, Graveland

Edgar, the Thin-Eager, arrives in Gloucester, some lifetimes late, lifts his head
above infant fog darkness, surveys the century, and the county, feeling festive.

Dumpland is pretty at Christmas
with litanies of lights, strung hand over fist over skips,
foiling the reverse sheen of the gorged land –
harbour of filthy thoughts and stay-at-home stench.
Touch me here, gulls. Flighty scavengers.

      Would you marry your king?
                Would you bury him?

By chance, Graveland is next to Dumpland
with bodies curated into slim subterranean cubicles
regular as the seasons and sealed
with intricate ground cover, busy lizzies, creeping phlox, bugleweed,
occasionally a rose. Bespoke animals, milling.

Edgar reverses deep into the Cotswolds, secures a private cot on the wold,
complete with candles and running slaughter and settles to sit out time.

Ring when you're home safe, Baby Scratch

The Mother General was taking the class that evening, novel in itself. We'd had a two-week break, for personal reasons of the usual Sister. Two latecomers, rough 'uns, come and sit beside me, ask if they can just listen. *Irritating.* I hiss to the girl, 'Why are you here? Who is it that you know who comes here?', sensing an agenda. 'Baby Scratch, who died,' she said. Wow, I thought, writing it down, but by this time her fella is telling the nun the whole thing – a veritable ballad of Baby Scratch –

'I knew Baby Scratch,' he said, 'her hair falling over. I walked her home that ugly night. *Johnny,* she said. I smiled. *Whiskey, you're the divil,* she said. Her laughter loud in the moon-spilt yard. Her hair falling over. I spit, and spat. A night of howdy singing, of fat talk, and chicken scraps, and a long-nosed man on a four-stringed guitar. Ah-ooo. I tried to catch her wrist, the little bone, the hopping vein. She snatched it back, a smile on her half-puckered rosebuddy mouth, running on, running in. *Don't ruck my dress, don't knock the door,* she said. *The folks'll wake,* she said. There weren't no folks, we knew, in this 'hossle' for girls like her, they didn't use a key, ah-ha. They didn't need a key. *That moon's in Africa, as well:* she cocked her head from the window above, sighed all dreamily. *Leave the door on the latch. There's another girl home after. Go now. There's someone else here after.* I could've, should've, pulled it to. Or rolled a rock across. The little tap, later, perhaps she thought it was me, her hair falling over. All pretty, the door left on the hook for another coming after. I knew Baby-Scratch-who-died' – he said – 'her hair falling over. The clackety-clack of her bangles and heels, her delly-cat wrists and ankles. I took her home that moon-spilt night. I should've stayed – I could've.'

I was taking notes but looked up to see MG, her eyes like an eagle's and next thing she was inviting him and the girl up to the front, for a prayer, hands held: 'Baby Scratch, beloved of us all,' she said. 'Your sweet fair hair, your cherub lips, and pretty birthmark. Have mercy, daughter, on your dispatcher, releasing you from evil. They meant you no harm. Surely, they didn't, little girl.'

And the whole class thrummed, *'Amen!'*

The Placenta Effect

A bonny burbling baby emerged in June
at the Harvingtons' house, at the edge of the wood.

'You need to eat the afterbirth,' the home midwife urged
(Lady Harvington looked limp and wrung, *wrong*): 'It'll pep you up.'

The Lord was hovering at the door, his whole life before and
behind him. He pooh-poohed Ms Grist, the doula, then slipped her

a crested plate to procure it for himself, the nutrient-dense
organ to be enjoyed at supper with bay and pepper,

sure to prolong his good looks and influence and, perhaps,
the doughty Ms Grist, too, might join him for a schooner of sherry

and the fruits of his wife's labour? He salivated. She agreed,
and bore him four more placentae in the next four years.

His wife declined.

[The undutiful and the beautiful]

The undutiful and the beautiful are introduced
does it develop?

The miner and the haulier hook up
do they talk shop?

The fat little rat and the thin little cat
what sprogeny?

autumns and rhythms and diddums
will they all pass, in time?

Ruskin's Contract

If he mashes your breasts with his caresses, Ma,
it won't go good for you. Little Ruskin was a worrier,

a careful guardian of his mother's ways.
The roughhousing of her various lovers

was what concerned him most. The beard rash
which raged for days and had him pounding

aloe vera for its soothing pith; applying it
with skilful little fingers. The lovers who left her

with white spots atop her tongue and a husky
voice from kissing: *Ma –*

he fixes lemons for a cut-sore-throat healing drink –
I'll look after you now. His silver fruit-knife

works away, slicing, flicking, with nimblest
delicacy and flair – a natural *noblesse*.

Mannequin, with the melancholy gaze –

you sit by my bed, a solicitous mother.
Though you never look at me
directly, I always wake to your pale blue
eyes, raking the air just above my head,

your pearl-peach complexion
pinking with concern for me,
your elegant neck tilted slightly
aside, to catch the doctor's footfall

on the stair.
           I will try to get better, Mannequin.
I will try to deserve your flawless love,
the riot of worries rolled beneath
your smooth chignon,

tumultuous anxieties bleeding
into your printed silks,
gorgeous with grief, which you control
superbly.

The Hold Days

All the lagging little children,
marked with measles and pox,
played in the red-brick courtyard,
alert for the ship's horn

to signal their return to the hold,
where Captains in stained uniforms
gave them ointment and diluted
rum, and told them winding stories

of the Cape, and sea monsters, and home.
They were invited up on deck, protected
by windcheaters and the ship's cook, who
saved biscuits for their broth and stroked

their curving shoulders and tiny hunchbacks,
bony as storks, and marvelled at their
white hair and pus-lined eyes. A kiss
at times escaped him for the smallest

one, for the smallest moment. *Forgive
me*, he muttered into a crusty scalp. *Bosun
Billy means no harm.* And cloudy eyes
flickered, holding his, with runtish hope.

Leperskin Coat

When I awoke, he was wearing his
leperskin coat, an elbow out
at the left, a wrist at the right, and
holes for England in his endless seams,
all for pity's sake.

I was used to his wiles, his Wednesday
face, wild 'clean-me' eyes, but this,
this.

Bleach, I said.

When you know someone's trying to force
your affection with cadaver-chic, and your heart's
half that way anyway but
you're not going to be made love's
fool forever. Victim to a pinch-me penchant.

He hangs a high-arm gap near to your lips,
your tongue could once-round it as quick as talk.
It looks salt. *Use bleach,* you repeat

but you're lost, his holes and cavings
calling you, unavoidable voids, violet
scrimshaw trouble, slinky invisible

vim, voile negativa, dripping
mangold, and any more than this

is always less.

A Whiff of Phosphor

I lay quiet by a nun while she divided air and parsed light
through her discarded veil. Without a wimple she brought to mind
a serious sweetshop proprietress I remembered from childhood, though
this nun smiled wide like one of those ninety-mile beaches in Oz.
I wanted to ask her 'How long?' but hesitated to have the conversation
become two-way, out of politeness, out-of-steam. The word XXXXXX kept
stuttering up in my throat and pole-vaulted my lips in the early hours,
towards three. 'That's one of my words, yes,' she acknowledged, smiling,
and balanced it between us on the unaccommodating bolster. There was
activity in the coal shed before dawn, rough-hewn voices, vocal
scowls, disembodied bluster and cussing. I got out of bed to lift the blind.
Light was peering in, amicably. He caught sight of the nun and bowed
                                                    before her,
draped and tiny. Then angled his arms and raised hands for her to begin
looping wool in huge skeins around his wrists until they became heavy and
he dropped them, loosing the spools. 'Unkempt like à Kempis!' she declared.
At Nocturns the new novices raced through the psalms raggle-tailed and
                                                    breathless,
clutching their flying habits as if cresting dunes in sight of the sea.
A lay-brother, like me, busied himself with balloons, inserting a £10
note into the neck of each one, before inflating them. 'A nominal
contribution,' he clarified. In the refectory we were given wine
in honour of the feast, viscous, ruby. Only Mother Prioress
gave the 'no' nod. We fifteen slumped collectively but consecutively as
a Mexican wave of torpor unmanned us. *Let the earth crack open and
crank forth a Saviour,'* one of the hermit nuns was moved to cry. The voice
seemed to come from the higher rungs of a stepladder and the sound
pulled at me, got inside my gut, like a baby's
cry. *'Your deliverance is near. I am your server for tonight. Angela
                              Superatus. Call me Sister.'*

How to Wring out Seven Devils

A swift rite left over from reforming days.
You have the best and most tempting heart, fugu
with fudge and cream. Unrealistically you resemble

the Arnolfini bride, silken but sluttish. Here's a conduit
for your gushing slaver. You have the look of a book of swatches
of indeterminate yellow, jejune as an ailing liver. I could roar,

you linger like a murderer, amazed at your clever no-clues.
Sadness switches sides, I thought I was on the other one
and they're scrawling something in freesia on the feature wall in Franglish.
Appetite sings off your gills. Why don't you give me a call.

Underland

(after that man 'Lewis')

Towards winter solstice, Alice
can no longer cope with groping down blind alleys,
being groped by creatures she doesn't
comprehend, in places obscure
to her. She has issues
with size, this human yoyo, no permanence and issues
between her thighs, no liniments. No
malice. Just a sweet intrinsic *no*
to everything. A refusal
to go along. This long winternight
is ritual to her, good rich black
fostering. Freedom
from his wittering.

Mole people

...feel where they need to be, feel they *are* where they need to be, have an instinct. When mewling mole infants, under mounds of loam, suffer mauling at the hands of young human males, mole matriarchs muse, and mind things differently; intuit, with tough muzzles and spade-hands, the humpbacked moon; conflate mountains with hills; mumble maudlin excuses for their babies' misfortunes – *imperative fallout* of their own chosen career – all hemmed into a corner, stitched up, in velvet.

Break Break Break

O rogue state which has dough-skin flapping about its neck full to capaz of blue whistled bigotry goitred with it and prorogued. Hounds leaving flour everywhere like maladjusted cooks rampaging in foreign cottages. Someone who shoots you down in your own slaughterhouse.

S.T. Coleridge Promotes His (Under) Wares

after – or before – 'Kubla Khan'

'A boob tube, or camisole, might suit,'
the gentle lingerie assistant advises:
'something which could be *flung up momently* –
silk and decorated with laurel leaves – a *cedarn cover*
for your *fertile ground*, which, together with a chic
teddy or merrywidow, will coyly cover
that deep romantic chasm. Our various ranges have
suspenders attached, or you could try
an unboned corset: all these will encourage
a mazy motion; our styles will encase you
in *holy and enchanted* lace; all you have to do is
rarify yourself with scent, something
churchy, so that like some *incense-bearing*
stately pleasure dome you'll evoke those
caverns measureless to man
and, like a prima donna *(woman wailing for her demon lover!)*,
can tantalise and *weave a circle round him thrice*
until, *seething, fed* on *honey-dew*,
he feels he's *drunk the milk of Paradise.*
Your lover, male or female, will adore you
as, sous-clothed and underdressed by us,
you'll slip adrift your silky froth and tread
this earth in fast thick pants.

That line you're looking at is *Xanadu.*'

Pastoral Moment

after Mary Jo Bang

A sharp lull on a sheep hill in Dorset:
frontdrop to artless coincidences & airless
confidences from a thrice-divorced roué
from Hull, originally; *milkspracht* & plausible.
I basket-weave pleasure
on a makeshift loom, schooled
to give as much as I get.
                           Blue-grey
mist palls the genteel hill, like a lady's
drawstring bonnet: candied evening light,
then a rush of soft-peeled dusk.

We eat cuttlefish off the bone, from a secret
compartment in the hamper, roasted
over charcoal. A leopard's head
on the catwalk translates into sleek chic
ears on my snood, & an ivory-plated choker.
A light hooked to the flame.
Staccato stars.

Not far away, in a Bournemouth drawing room,
a wronged woman wrings her hands,
dips fists in rosewater & elaborates lists.
A screen in the corner shows classic Hardy
with round-vowelled milkmaids & joking
yokels. She'll bemoan her outdated life,
while half-attending to the muted drama,
& scribbling down names of dresses like *Milly-Joanne*.
Wouldn't it be better to think he had gone to war,
she'll flash in her tarnished cage.

I call him my 'trumpet-major,' enjoy
cut-throat frissons of Jurassic passion
& ask about her at intervals. *Ask her
to forgive me.* Here is no real light.
Only hard mouths, hands, & jungle
hunger – & knowing
that nothing, often, can be reversed.

The next day,

chipmunks gathered outside in the forest to the back of the house, coming right up to the French windows and French-kissing them so that I could only see rows of tiny black holes and pointed pink tongues. I was hiding from a lady in a crocheted cap whom I'd heard storming past the front gate screaming *I'm not leaving till I've seen her.* The light outside in the forest was a uniform green, limey, hanging in curtains from lichened twigs, trapping gobbets of sun which tried unsuccessfully to turn it to gold. I put my back against the door, feet to the chest-of-drawers for ballast. I couldn't believe I'd left the front door unlocked and all the blinds open at the front, after coming in hot from church. I listened for movement in the house, thought I heard furniture being shifted, treasures being tweaked, imagined them being sucked out through the unlocked door. Eventually I unlatched the French windows, shoving aside eager furry flesh, and ran towards the town, arriving surprisingly quickly at a cobbled street where everything was olde-worlde, lakey-districty. I just wanted a common-or-garden shop, for a snack, for phone credit. In desperation I headed into a slightly crooked boutique, hung with muscular sweaters and gabardine macs. The shoplady looked surprised and then delighted as she gave me a nineteenth-century look and her face dimpled and wreathed as she tried to hand me the change belonging to another customer. I demurred, nodding towards a bebagged gentleman behind me. *Blimey! You're right – and honest*, she beamed in a Dickensian way. I asked for top-up and she asked if she could measure me around the breasts. *Not looking for clothes*, I said nervously. *I won't bite!* she laughed, like a brook speeding and breaking over rocks. I wondered, if I gathered up all my courage, took deep green breaths and went back, maybe calling via the church to warm myself at the candles, if everything would be all right, if I could ever be chipper, or monkly, again.

Refract: Blackbird

Coloured one by one, only to fall apart,
pines and balsams have thrown out all
their hundred grievances.
The forest suddenly rains

mix of noble fir, incense, cedar;
a specific wind visits with a breath.
Red-winged blackbird
rises uneasily from the forest-floor

with a wreath of thin-walled nuts.
Buttercups paint the gold off a nest.
Horseflies shoo people back
from yellow cloud banks,

clearing and refusing the area.
Coloured one by one, only to fall apart.

Moon Rising

Girl, grandmother, and mother live where the sun is sick and gives off scurfy light. Their men have perished, the whole line gone to ground: a frazzled wire. The three women train themselves like mercury to wait.

Mornings drop like dead gulls the first year. In spring a pedlar brings a holy picture of three figures – Mary and Joseph in Jerusalem where they've found the Child, three days lost. 'Wait,' says the grandmother. 'I'll take it, in memory of those gone. Perhaps the presence of the icon will lend light.'

The pedlar catches answering light in the young girl's eye, throws in six pebbles: *'Wait to see if they bring luck, three and three,'* he chants: *'who knows the lack-charm places where they've been, where others may have gone.'*

Mornings limp like sick magpies. Another year. The girl strokes stones as months make up a year twice more till she is ten; palms their ochre light; scrazes them across red soil; gauges weights while grandmother intones petitions to the Three-in-One. The girl sees her mother changing, her smiles gone, her tongue spiked with jet which snags the failing rays. The girl learns where to go, what to do, to shelter from the jagged light.

Grandmother shuns mother; for three months stays mute, turned to the wall, her mettle gone. The girl rinses pebbles, rubs them, plays ducks-and-drakes, waits till autumn's ghost marries winter the following year.

Fish bloat, fabulous with roses, the pedlar's sixth year. Women eye a scarlet moon; each other; say, 'Let's wait.' The girl hones pebble-gems, hums to menfolk gone, hangs a necklace round the grandmother's picture, on her plot.

Towards solstice, she loses focus, secretes blood; her cheeks flare alight. Some sightings of the pedlar.

People murmur; and black scales, they swear, flake from the mother's tongue – she's heard to cry, 'We can again be three!'

Priests turn up soon after, wearing black, probing into years gone by. They question women under oath; name and bridle culprits where they can.

Three times they light upon the mother; three times the girl says – 'Wait!'

little one

the baby arrived with stitched lips
no matter how hard the midwife tried
she couldn't undo the stitches
and, shrugging, handed her over
for the needle-eyed mother
to see to

lemonjim hour: *brittle england*

the muse, here to amuse, brings a clock.
my hands and brain are chapped from taking her notes.
glimquist and sunkissed on a burgundy chaise longue
she turns phrase after phrase on the lathe of her tongue
until, fluted and threaded, drilled, joisted and planed, she produces
five flights of solicitor's banisters to snake down the staircase,

                                                hemming me in and

she is truth-pillowing everything out so that I'm breathing as
shallow and stinky as rockwater, anemone-blind, choking on her alien
mouthwash as she bats me from pillar to post, copper-manic,
feeding me what she calls *ilk milk*, squeezed from white cliffs of dover,
she a sovereign autonomous rose, till she drops like a poppy, one ochre
petal for each bong of the clock at tea time, drumming the carpet
with glee

Apple Snow

Once again Mr Grandet, my neighbour, has left me the gift of one of his daughters on the doorstep. This morning it's the big-chinned baby, in an end-times romper-suit. She swings a berried switch of something like rowan in her left fist, and her limbs feel chill to the touch as I scoop her up, and scan the street: dozens of front gardens studded with fruit trees. Why can't he simply leave me a box of damsons or plums, or just a few crab apples, I wonder. The toddler, inside, carries out a number of rituals – kitchen, bedroom, bathroom – then plants her legs in opposing quadrants of the Mondrian hearth-rug and settles to a game of spell-making (or whatever it is she does), grabbing a pair of drumsticks, and crooning and rocking. I return to the kitchen where I feel like I've been preparing the same whey-coloured breakfast for weeks, years, it seems. When I go back to the living room, the infant appears to have grown, and I catch her peeking at a training bra underneath her top, and pouting her lips. *Look, Ma!* she calls out. I have a rule that she doesn't call me 'Ma', but, when I remind her, she goes all faux-affectionate and straddles my calves with her warming and not inconsiderable thighs, saying *Mumsie-Wumsie*. Then she offers me three wishes, relinquishing the drumsticks and wafting the rowan switch in front of me, its sequin berries winking. I wish for 'music' and the piano starts up a piece in E minor, causing the air to tremble and divide like slivers of silver jelly, and threatening to play itself into tears or torpor. I am contemplating my other wishes – perhaps Mr Grandet could be liberated early from the jam factory, and hurry home to collect his charge? – when I receive a phone call from a solicitor informing me that a decision has been made (after much shuffling of official forms), that the girl will live with me, *hereinafter*, while she occupies herself in *compiling an index of domestic magic*, and will answer to the ancient English name *Wigga*. In return for board and lodgings she will source a daily breakfast of fruit, variously foraged and prepared: whiskey-poached pears, plum fritters; devilled figs; pert mounds of blancmange topped with apple snow.

Merry Foreigners in our Morning

a golden shovel

> Merry foreigners in our morning,
> we laugh, we touch each other,
> are responsible props and posts.
> – Gwendolyn Brooks

In the spirit of saintly old Thomas More, we shall meet merry
in heaven, our souls spliced from our limbs – now foreigners –
our graveclothes curling away from us, like proud lilies in
a suburban kitchen, the familiar waft of bacon in our
nostrils, pulled wide-awake, our soul-nostrils greeting the faux-morning.
And every time we turn to check out potential companions we
encounter, instead, our reflections in a sliding door, and laugh.
It's not curious that we should look hindward as we
attempt to acclimatise, or that our former porky lives touch
as we walk lockstep in rough brotherhood, seeking each
other, even as each acknowledges long-stored unknowing of that other,
and our warmed-through grief, and how our snivelling elbows'
                                                      remnants are
so out of sync, so class-untrue, and how we are responsible
only for our brains and our will, the eventual consequences being
                                                        mere props

which turn up independently and
switch us into silly signposts

golden opportunity, wet streets

give his side a golden opportunity to move
each passing minute seemingly misses one
– if you have
anaconda, or ball python, pine –

opportunity to read what everyone
open in the mouth and good
could see. For one year flowers shone
blooming in Sweden at the end of May.

Assigned to the city of Spokane,
we are over the charred or crumbling
rain-wet street. I stood at the War
(for seconds). Lilies sued for peace

each passing minute seemingly missing one
while lilac snow milled wisdom in city ruins.

ii
oulipo yew engenders TT strop

oily graveside glove shunted. Motto pops.
Cone shape sings, mining tissue
of hay – vie
a dapple, a coin, a thorny *no*.

In pop tryout, a doter overeaten (why?)
a hotdog mound, phone nite,
curdle of slow – nearer – eyes, hoof, nose;
glib moon, dew nines; anatomy hefted.

And, if egoists speak no cot, they
hover, chartered, or – alembic wren-rug –
retrain tweets: the raw iota dots,
forced sons, idle lies. Faeces pour

canapé sighs, gene-slimy, semi-nosing.
Limned owls will leach, ruin Midi sow's icy tit.

iii
golden streets

give his side a golden move,
each passing minute one.
Have
anaconda, or pine.

Opportunity to everyone
open in the good
could see, for one shone
blooming in Sweden at the May.

Assigned to the Spokane,
we are over the crumbling
rain-wet street. I stood War
(for seconds). Lilies. Peace.

Each passing minute, one.
While lilac snow milled wisdom ruins.

iv
Give his golden move,

each one.
Or pine.

To everyone
the good
could. One shone
blooming in the May.

The Spokane,
we, the crumbling
rain-wet, stood War.
Lilies. Peace.

Minute one.
While lilac wisdom ruins.

v
Forgive his golden move –

one
pine.

Everyone
good
one shone
in the May.

Spokane
the crumbling
stood War.

Peace.
One
lilac wisdom ruins.

vi
Move one pine.

Everyone good shone.
May, Spokane crumbling.
War. Peace. One.

Ruins.

Filth

(after ten days)

Mult mult mult mult. Orange light
invades the street. Prayer is hung
in quartos. Idle eyes calculate the damage
of ten nights since his long blue-suited limbs
unfolded from the carapace sepia interior
of a 1950s sedan, his pointy face
anxious and private. A pall of tragedy
about his ears. How he approached
the front door where mild suburban weeds started up –
doubled wires dipped in violet. 'Bella Langley?' he probed.
'Some news of your son.' Mult. The pipit face broke
into ricochet smiles and frowns. Mult? 'Come in.'
The soft pandered atmosphere made way
as the deranged house urged him in. Doors
double-locked. Curtains folding him into promises
and blood oaths. Silence burrowed through the neighbours'
walls. No one emerged. Nothing until the sirens, the lights.
A blue suit stained. A caged bird. Microbial activity.
Sympathy cards. Mult mult mult. Mass-produced
prayer. Sepia photographs under rank multiplying
headlines. Belladonna. Appallment. Violet light masters
every unshaded window in the street. Mult.

Hopeless on Hope Street

Hope lopes along like a bandit.
Mrs Molesworth looks sceptical.
Wants the streets cleaned up. What a pass
when every low-looking male
can stuff municipal waste bins with white stuff
to believe in. Outside the barber's, Hope
combs a moustache and finishes with a gloss
of wax, taking care to equalise left and right.
Mrs Milkwater expostulates that low-looking
girls can air their toilette in public as if
at a show. She gathers up Hope's implements
and secretes them in her handbag like hotel
courtesies. Mannequins stand in protest
outside the town hall, 17 abreast, reaching
as far as Bell Street. Their gaze favours
the right side where shop windows
are spritzily lit and sparsely furnished.
The man watering the Council flower baskets is dazzled,
transported to the Russian ballet, light on his feet
as he leaps past, illegally snagging begonias
from solicitors' window boxes. Hope stifles
a cough, lifts a muffler. Mrs Merryweather
de-steams her glasses and considers the ways
in which peace will come, by water
and by blood. False sunlight falls hard.
Hope struts on high heels. The street
is busier now. Flesh in flux. The evening
is a belter. Lights stuck on red. People singing
hymns at the zebra. Some men are cursing
their lives while women wonder about
crossing. Some set off together; sometimes
they drift back, swaying.

Elf Sex

Lush primroses: lushest along the verges
like custardy stars, long constellations
leading to the dell, where bodies loll
in hollows. Springtime trysts, extramarital
elves, *malelvolence*, elfin hanging from horse
chestnut chandeliers, dozens of teenagers lured
across the lane, dazzled by lights,
the odd errant housewife.

Eyes in a Whirl

On the nth of suck-tuber, an ounce and a pinch of thyme,
two mothers in the same gown of blue burlap,
were passing the new pig-five block near the park
on the bus. Eyed each other: *Get off and lark it!*

They gathered musk and bourses, eggy,
and peeped themselves on two flues. Text-fawning,
they hit the egg-sack. Summer was not sealing the gorse
but an old shrew, with cool enough plinth to smuggle

to Ipswich, laughed off neonatal silk. A stud
cajoled them with a mouthful, and Winnie,
the second mother, free-ranging the cursed time,

rolled over in lavender, staggered up smelling of roses.
You wronged my ex, claimed Dr Mitry, her co-player,
sore lover. *So pin it and draw it, and scram!*

Cockaigne

after Edward Elgar

The smack of *wet* and *loud* in London town;
a puff of steam and flap of fog; a hoop, a top;
a bowler, boater, merry-widow hat.

Cheeky streetboys – cocks of the walk – hawking wares,
chasing dogs and horse-drawn cabs, bobbing, weaving, alive
to the rollicking circus. A carnival of sins of the chirpy
chuckling kind. A cackle or two. Cockles; eels; steak pie.

Round the corner a cockade – brass band! – and London's heart
swells. A man would be a brute not to stand and salute
the Sally Army, and now the soldiers… All still to play for.

And now, again, old London *bustles*
– as fast as modern ladies abandon
theirs, for sleeker silhouettes,
and 'Votes for Women!', and cycling
in Hyde Park; a march to Hampstead Heath
in mud or powdery dust. Here's raucous singing,
all the craic – 'Down at the Old Bull & Bush'.

Take a peek in the park for views of licence –
a line of nuns who 'strip stark-naked for their play'.
A peal of bells; and lovers loiter, mutually appealing.
Wide green spaces unravel, and it's for all the world
like Malvern, Malvern, hills and sky
and running wild with kites. Intertwined

with this, the filigree circus – and rivers of milk
and beer… Champagne! A belter of a city.
Cockney savvy veering into sheer noblesse.

Medieval England speeded up to a melee of sharps
and toffs and old cockers. Cockaigne. Our little Eden,
burgeoning with pride and never shy of its underside.
The orchestra blazes – this London, this drug.

Note: The detail of the nuns who 'strip stark-naked for their play' derives
from 'The Land of Cockaygne', a medieval poem by a Franciscan friar,
describing this fictional land; 'rivers of milk' are also associated with
this subversive and mythical place of plenty, which by Elgar's time had
become whimsically identified with London.

April on the Chiltern Line

ride ride the moonslung sea
slide along the chalk-crumbed
crumbling blackthorn
hedges hooped and braided
feather-touch and tail-thick
April whites.
White skip, white trip
playing on the
tree-tips, milk-dripped
dribbling, sloe-quick
slow, swallowed up in hazy
snow-blur; blow.
Syllables of random
petal, hiccupping
in gateways. Walls,
scribbled on by toddlers –
undulating pages
wriggling free: blossom
snagging on the old beards
straggling the verges.
Blossom like a woman
cancelling her beauty
– drifted flower-curls.
Racing spirogyra!
Syllabubs unfolding
townward,
mixing in with cherry
piping – pavements –
coconut in icing
twinned with pink;
carabang, cara-
bang, carabang, with

a cartoon screech
new to the field which
we've just said goodbye to,
lurching off again, strangers
shifting, backwards, sideways
settle to the hum and
sway, ravished by the bride-
al spray, foaming, poeming,
breaking out of line-
ing, bent on riding
moonwrung moonhung
skidded-in-a-spinning
snowstrung sea

Wood Magic

after Elgar's *Cello Concerto in E Minor, op. 85*

> *smiling Edwardian afternoons… all gone, gone, lost forever*
> (J.B. Priestley, *The Linden Tree*)

Skewered on chords of war, the century stumbles.
Mother Europe loosens her shawl, frets
at her best glass shattered, her petticoats stained.

In our bowl of hills, we hear it all, far off, back and forth.
My husband cocks his hat, turns up his collar
and the volume, strains eyes and ears towards the Channel.

Pizzicato artillery weaves with cries of gulls.
Seventeen million lost. In these hills, in chartreuse
shadows, souls drag their heels, unresting.

Our dallying, doilied afternoons, gashed open, gone.
Wraiths in chains wander the woods,
whispering in fritillaried hedges
and among the Queen Anne's lace.
England, my lady… What frolics, what sore limbs.
There's a rampage of glad-ragging grave-digging sprites…
My darling melody… A girl shins up an apple tree —

God, this is plangent — tell us your plan, gents! —
gone, long gone. Lost. A thin silver dolour
winds itself through the season.
My husband is writing wood magic. He whistles.

Master Grief straps on a knapsack,
grabs meat pie for a picnic,
still tipsy from yesterday's pale ale.
A brawler, he's up before dawn.

I see pinpoints of light.
Dear Normandy lit.
I smell linden, honeysuckle.
I know skin.

Now, Mother Europe, it's time:
look again to your shawl – to your stars…

Note: The phrase 'wood magic' is from Alice Elgar's diary, describing her husband's late works.

proggle

after John Clare

summers blue caps in the corn   bumbarrel babies barely grown
and eyes all over the shop   clink and bandy lasts for ever
john barleyshock   mean clown clanking the rosy sleeping boy
by glibbed sexpool and fox loth to gin

mary fallingfromatree unfancy fruit   round grounded
looks up at me I soodling

cran cheeks and tongue cooled in cressy pond draughts
my lips bold-wasping her crimson cherries
glegging spinner of me   bliss in her apron
ah august ago, ago

Melody's Meadow

There are flowers out in my head that are still bulbs in the everyday world, tight-lipped. There are always other beds to consider apart from this one in the middle of a meadow, canopied with biblical hawthorn, which we've made our own. Beds within beds, cooled then warmed, decoded. A piano in the hedge, stuffed with old newspapers, which plays when I am asleep though I try to rouse myself to see if it could be a mouse or a melodeon. My parents visiting again, first thing, this time checking why we haven't got curtains, or walls. I try to tell Dad about the piano, he would be tickled, but my pronunciation is way off and he doesn't recognise the words emerging like aubergine. My mother keeps going off by herself, looking for more modern meadows, with self-cleaning daisy carpets and colour badgers. There are at least a dozen other children claiming her care, looking anxious and reedy. My brain is stuffed with laburnum blooms, ravishing but poisonous. We turn to pray and two of my nephews light honey-candles and act as acolytes. One overacts. A sailor on a quest for enough sky to make himself a pair of trousers drops by, but the steel grey heavens strengthen a tendency to introversion, and no one entertains him. One of the sisters baptises herself 'Xenophobia'. He asks another sister to marry him and she quizzes him about his clothing allowance. Half-a-dozen brothers scrap for his compass. By this time it's evening and the hour to draw the veil over the bed, twiggy and fragrant. My beloved turns to bestow a kiss but I snatch it from him prematurely, green and unsucculent. I leave it with the sailor, a morsel next to his nightcap. The day has not been as fruitful as others in the meadow but at least there were no marauders, and only a scattering of goats. Two of my brothers shout out, claiming to know where we are.

Leaving Glawdom by night –

dressed glam in twisted serpent
bangles and a sly mothy stole
I set off north by north-east
for seven leagues until I met

the sea, arching Atlantic
coastline, white foam, high noise
and 3 youths, smiling, yelling
into the wind, selling

apples, peddling riddles.
I asked them how many years –
did they know – they called back
dozens; how far out to sea –

America; where the treasure
was – *in silver conches hanging
from the wreck which pirates
ransacked last November.*

I thanked them, pretending
to understand, and bought 3 russets,
rough and tawny, slid them
inside my knapsack and continued

south by south-west for thirteen
furlongs until I met
an old forest creaking
with gold and auburn baubles –

hummingbirds attending –
and squirrels swivelling rich trinkets
till the branches seemed to dance
and I thought I understood

and glanced around for maidens
I could quiz, but there were none
and I shrugged off my bag,
kicked loose my sandals, gripped moss

between my toes and smelled
woodsmoke, half-baked apples, saw
the whole darn forest
tonguing devilish

orange flames and I tried
to plot the hopping curlicue
edges with my pencil and my
compass and where were

those mystic maidens who could guide
and give me wisdom and suddenly
I heard them laughing, high-stepping
in a glade, they were rifling

plated conches full of treasure,
dangling bracelets from their teeth
jewels banging on their chins
and I looked aghast – me a ghost,

half-rubicund and silt with ash –
what could I ask?

Nympholepsy

after Edward Lear

Unbuckle your ukulele
and let us hear you hum;
unfed, you'll never get your grub
unless we hear you strum.

He paused and drew her from his pack
let slip her velvet drape
and greedy eyes drank deeply
as he fingered her elegant nape.

Mahogany, magnificent,
like no creature so much as a cat,
with its guts strung out on its poker-straight tail –
where *did* you, sir, get *that*?

All the time he played, they were restless:
What a mistress, he has his fill –
see the way his hand fits into her waist
and the way she draws his skill!

They jollied more coins in their pockets
led on by the ale and the air
and just the thought that, if he played some more,
they would know why they were there –

would know, would know.
They would know why they were there.

Mablethorpe-by-Bea, 1933

A pink frill at the edge of the ocean
as the sun dipped near the end of that week;
limbs pitted and creviced with salt,
twice-sabled by sand, and mild sun.

You haven't a notion, she said.
I haven't an ocean, I heard.
She tipped and propelled me towards dark home.
Away from the lingerers and pork-pie

hatters and eaters, the sausage-limbed
daughters, lapping up the last of it,
the little days of September, the pangolin
dew-drop days, everything scaled and gold.

She fastened the frill on my bonnet,
tucked in the plaid rug at the sides
of my thighs, spun my chair round on two of its wheels –
Whee, she said, *whee, Bea, we're free!*

This Heart
(after Kim Addonizio)

This cancelled cheque stub.
This ruby nightdress,
flammable/inflammable.

This pack of spare Catherine wheels.
This sack of reindeer antlers – kindling
dried to tinder – this pot of glue.
This old lover's glove, stitched leather.
This mechanical sunshine.
This front parlour for aunts
backbiting while they sip Assam.
This madly blossoming plum tree.
This coal mine, abandoned in 1984.
This crimped envelope, played with, not sent.
This hillock overlooking the Atlantic
in the evening, lambs blarting.
This medlar missing from a medieval tapestry.
This Montessori experiment. Car boot sale.
This click when the box is shut.
This poem begun again.

This poem begun again. This nightmare –
lurching down a hill without brakes.
This royal wedding, with gilt napkin ring.
This four-chambered castle, draughty,
timeshared. This pump. Pimp.
Pampered infant, stubborn-cheeked.
This alleyway for unseemly loitering.

This bag of chips, over-vinegared.
This carrier-bag, stuffed with old calendars.
These urgent messages.

The Spoiler

There is a Spoiler
who stalks the house at dawn
snuffling out sweet truffles
of success, wherever he may find them.
His soft snout he
bruises
behind chair backs
and magazine racks
under piano lids and fridges
and unattended table
tops: to suck them out
complete. With a filmy
yellow eye he looks them over,
plays desultory keepy-uppy
between muscle-corded thigh
and hoof, then, with a twist
of the same, squishes them.
Success's smell is sharp upon the air
for just a moment, then recedes.
Though he doesn't seem discerning
he usually has a nose for those
best things of the day before:
some crystalline creative act;
small victory over sin – a preference
for the virginal success – bracts infurled
against a globed corolla –
due to drive joy dazzling through the veins
of the achiever, when, come daylight,
it will leaf-bloom-fruit uniquely.
The Spoiler has an instinct:

sniffs, quizzes, lobs, and squishes.

Louder than 'Jerusalem'

I am the holder of the negative / gathering up dissent / collecting censure /
attending to the underside / the other point of view / I cannot help /
but pick up cavils / which have clattered to the concrete / and from the
carpet unsnag / strands of carping / I see insult and spittle / and soak up
shame / adroitly I absorb / defamation and reviling / cold-shouldering /
backbiting / belittlement / (I've made a list / and ticked them off) /

In the carnivals of congratulation / I listen for lament / in swollen
exaltation / on days of celebration / a whispering hollows out my joy /
resounding louder than / 'Jerusalem' /

If I notice some small discarded item / evidence of dirty dealing or a lady's
garment, say – / not quite in keeping with the tenor of the day – / I hold
it blushing tucked beneath my arm / until the owner comes to claim it / I
pine to be swept along on a flower-strewn float / up up up with height and
hilarity / I scarce know what to do / with all I carry / I have some more /
in storage / I hold this pole

Rise and Fall

I like Hopkins, I said, shyly.
'God's Grandeur... Pied Beauty...
Felix Randall... Henry Purcell...
Hurrahing in Harvest...
Inversnaid... Ribblesdale... The Leaden Echo
and the Golden Echo – *Spelt from Sibyl's Leaves!* – '

'Indeed!' The Oral Examiner lifted her hand,
then let it drop, and brush – like ah! plushy-velvet –
against my marks sheet. 'Perhaps now
you'd like to tell us why?'

Even to Kind-hearted Men

Think of things from your brother's perspective;
sneak your soft foot in his size seven shoe.
Take a vantage point from behind the sofa;
observe your self, uncertain and probing,
that broken-fawn look and that motion-blur –
pink ballerina endlessly spinning
on the tip of every decision,
never outright or clear. Then you will learn,
as I have now learned, that seeking to please
pleases no one. Unshouldered selfhood
weighs others down. And sickly things, even
to kind-hearted men, and boys, exude spices
inciting them to urgent clarity, cuffs and fresh blood.

Capt

Bent over in a cat-smelling space,
Witch Isobel flexes her fingers,

rolls her swan-like, uncurls crabbed
toes. The church has tried to curb her

activity, hobble the hares of good-doing
she set coursing from her hermit's cave.

But lime toads, balled dormice, and all kinds
of kindly wildlife plead for her outside

her cell. *She only ever thought of
others*, they cried (even those who'd suffered).

*She only ever sought vengeance on mothers
twisting their offspring, priests damning*

their charges. And her shining skin, crooned
one elegant weasel to himself, *is handsome*

as honey. All the creatures of the forest
ululated; their lament reached the dew-wet

fields at the boundaries, clogged with ragwort.
Witch Isobel draws in her fingers, relaxes

her neck, re-curls her toes. Riding a fug
of euphoria, she awaits news of the dour

Monsignor, expected Sunday, from far off,
whose horse is said to be ailing, himself thrown.

Wing-Broke Angel

A wing-broke angel, prone on the lemon laminate floor
of the library, stunned and starry-eyed. I admire the hulk
of the one unbroken wing rising like surf
from young unmuscled scapular bone.

A total waste of money, one Midlands matron
vents. And *Is this room all there is?*
from another punter. January sunset burns livid
against front-facing 'Spring Reads'; seraph breaths

grow sparse. The very first time
an angel has visited: no protocol to speak of.

Book of Blue

Mid to ¾ way through a gold and crimson century
a monk, glad from Nocturns, committed himself
to fix a thousand words, all slippery and impure
for secular posterity. His papery hands illuminated
each one, extemporising nipples, buttocks, quim,
with quick strokes of a vigorous quill. Ignoring strictures
of obedience, he privately celebrated created beauties,
praising the bawd. Apathy kicked in at 666.
The great Bede himself was piqued. And Father Abbot's
eyes – averted – watered.

Hyacinthoides non-scripta

Calverkeys, wood bells,
campanula, glockenblume,
– or just a common bluebell

Beryl-the-Peril Bluebell

Tell blue, you flower:
tell a querulus of best
blue to the flat white
meadow stuck in
picture-book reverie.

Stalk joy with your stem
and your airy, fairy bell.
Stick your pistils out
and, in that shot-silk thimble,
ring like hell.

Compact

The mirrors of Devon are devilish,
flipping you stormy-side up, rendering you
vamp, ramping up your beauty levels
till you burst, scorched, out the top.

Midlands mirrors have a patina, an
easy-at-home cast which lasts
and tints your glass with rose, kindling
kindness and tricking you

to domestic hubris. Northern mirrors
house fey shadows, bouncing faces and
bodies back at you, till, left to right,
the mercury cringes with ghosts, and you blister.

From Rivariations – Leam, Ouse, Derwent

[Lovely the Leam and her sisters]

Lovely the Leam and her sisters
milling through Midlands
watermeadows. Broadbacked
and elegant, halving the Spa town.

There was a story in childhood
of three daughters of one family,
adrift in a boat, lost. Leam lowered
her gaze and mourned. *Hypocrite river.*

THE OUSE IS MY (UNEXPECTED) HOME

I slip into the day as into swish silk.
Up before anyone, digging out morning's
moist newness like truffles. Green prickling
my nose, sharp as thorn. I head down the slope.
Hop. Down by the apple trees, down by
the apple trees. Skip.

The water is plated, a table set for tea.
One little white teacup for you, my dear.
A trembling, almost transparent, slice
of angel cake.

Icy green slink – *oh why did you* –
fugitive flurry, rattlesnake breath.
How roomy here, in this black heart.

Mr Derwent

How d'you do, my rushing gent, tawny-capped,
whiskers bristling, up at Howden, busy about
a northern agenda, along steep corridors,
ten thousand items to see to, circling the scree
and sparing a word to court the lady scar. Debrief
at Hathersage, healing rush down through
Matlock. Thick oak valleys. You try to hold it back
but you break out with such a brown surge.
Whip, slap. Mutate, flower into cotton and silk.
I follow in my head, on, on through rock
and lime and moor, always forward
with canny grit; brief circuits, but blunt as a tongue.
The wind confounds you at Ambergate.
I spent two years trailing you
then wonder where you went.

Diagnosis

He said he had rotting hair,
falling teeth, greasy skin,
a dowager's paunch, flat creviced feet,
halitosis, a boxful of ticks, myopia,
lack of confidence with strangers, tendencies towards incontinence…

'And the dog,' the vet enquired: 'You think
all this is affecting the dog?'

Cold-Room George

His old mother hides him in the pantry,
his floury belly half-heartedly coated

with breadcrumbs, jowls gravid
with jellied gravy, tagliatelle

and segments of tangerine. Morning
to evening he plays with the toy air.

Marshalls soldiers from cut bread,
parades them, pa-rum-pa-pum-pum.

Arranges triage, and first-aids the injured
with marmalade and marshmallows.

Awards royal tarts as honours,
jam shining like jewels.

While all the while the father
bellows *Hen!*, shaking his boots

overhead (fee-fi-fo-fum)
You're mollycoddling him,

you'll make him soft.
Daft egg.

Down Among the Dead Birds

Sick Bird Ode

1. Electrified blackbird: red for a split second before feathers spit & sizzle
2. Fried wagtail, marinated in tamari, with a nod to ginger & chocolate; best enjoyed with Merlot
3. Reformed robin, cut cute into heart shapes
4. Humungous hummingbird, gastric ring vibrating, in the dead head of a promiscuous foxglove
5. Salty wren, round & around the globe in a boat
6. Two-a-penny sparrow, hanging its costly dead head
7. Daily nightingales, disturbing the piece
8. Craven raven, blenching
9. Crooked rook, two up, two down, one across
10. Whore hawk, an eye on the hummingbird
11. Limping swift, sore thumb
12. Difficult swallow, oesophageal clench
13. Blind eagle, hawk-eyed, her desire running after the man. *Ave. Ave.*

Tailpiece: fool girl, good gull

A scold tale of an Irish Ma, a bold tale like Brian Boru, seething with reason & riddled with sense, an old story, folded in two, a Sabbath rest punctured with law & lore, rolled into a ball to be kicked by princes to kingdom come. Charming. Holed-up, giddy & goldy-locked, she's sold down the river by dolts.

Downsizing

The experts flew in on Monday, white-shirted, corner-perfect.
I saw one engaged in irony just outside the lift, peeling,
with her bare palms, layers thick as plywood from the walls
and doors. A pliant assistant with perpendicular red hair
was noting down stray rhetorical tics from passing staff,
green pen flicking back and forth like a mating grasshopper.
My cousin who works on the ground floor, in 'Village 66'
(streetside), said that they stayed for a week, white clouds of them
skittering whenever you opened a door or a cupboard. No one
knew what they ate. Only – after they'd left – the fridges were empty,
some staff had disappeared, and some of those
remaining had lost centimetres of bone
from their spines, and will.

Champagne

When old Mr Spence telephoned in January to ask if I'd pick up some 'fancy cleaner' on my way in, to bring up the blue tiles in his bathroom to look like 'Etruscan mosaics' or 'the turquoise Aegean' while I scrubbed his back, I resigned. I'd been restless for a while, negotiating the rising silt of travel brochures, drafts of letters with my name scrawled passim; champagne flutes containing dregs of fruity cocktails, emeralds of mould.

I went to the agency and told them I wanted to retrain as a bus driver.

'But you're a natural cleaner.' Giselle at the front desk averted an anxious eye to my onscreen profile. 'Home help. Carer.'

'I'm not a social worker.' (Or Turkish-Bath attendant, I wanted to say.) She bit her lip. 'Our older clients like you.'

'It says in your window "BUS DRIVERS WANTED URGENTLY".'

My New Year belligerence didn't abate and within the hour I was stepping up onto a *Sorry, I'm-Not-In-Service* number 78 for my first training session. Garage-fresh, a whiff of ammonia lingering in the aisle. I sensed tension dropping from me. Pulled open the driver's gate and let it swing against my middle with pleasing weight.

Winter diamonds winked on the girders at the depot entrance, made me think of Paris, the Eiffel Tower. I leant back in the leatherette seat; felt a rush as I tested the pedals.

EDWARDIANA

An inch or two skimmed from her twill skirt
and the day shaped perfectly in her head:
seamless tennis, swimming, a cycle down the lane
and up, a rondeau of elevenses with aunts,

then two loops unhooked from her corset
for patriotic postprandial singing around the piano,
the map of England shaved perfectly on her head.

Strong tea in thin-lipped china, a cake-stand charged
with madeleines and buttered teabreads – mountains! –
shared perfectly by her bed: a long ramble
with a newish lover, in slant-lit gardens, mallow

weighting the air and, under row after row
of high-arching yew, yards and yards
of shadow waiting perfectly up ahead.

O Respectability

Your lemon-clean hands, your exact
half-moons. Your front-room
manners. Your surfaces purged
of paper. Your embargo on books
with their runaway pages.
Your meticulous regard
for appearances, cultivated
from Sunday to Sunday. Your clarity
about all that is licit, your unerring
thumb in the manual of mores.
Your restraint, your face turned against
what would be simple or pleasant, a devoted
minister at the altar. Your faultless flower-
beds, paved patios, weed-treated verges.
Your topiary, trained into ramparts
and turrets. Your commitment
not to stray into tropical flowers or flippant foliage
and to leave all that for heaven. Your friendship
with the tyrant tidiness, at ease.
Your generous offering of your children's
spirits as fuel. O my enemy.
Let them learn hereafter. Your soft civility and
aristocratic instinct for duty. Your
implacability. Your congenial face,
hemmed skirts, best coat. Your meal-
plan, life-plan, retirement-plan, funeral-
plan, your crystal glasses and grades of china
and cheese. O my enemy, your love of enemas.
Your unfailing response at funerals, balled
handkerchief out of sight, and your discretion
at weddings, tongue in check

about the bride's peccadilloes. Your unfaltering step.
Your adherence to rulefulness and no
shilly-shallying. Your insurance. Your fidelity
to who you are. Your fixed hue. Your blendable
dependable face. Your being welcome at every
event. Your never being caught
out. Your lack of shade.
Your true blue heart.
Your polished brass. Your nets.
Your drawers of ironed linen.
Your front room always ready
Your paying your dues
and respects
to the world.
Your history.

You're history.

Plumber's Mate: 98

Dumb you, you gave consent for that first fling
(damn you, for my assent to that First Thing).
Deadheaded spring, spring-headed Daddy,
spring-loaded king, with all the trimmings,
zinging – decades of me anonymous in odour,
hue, punctilious freeloader you,
plucking men from my lap –

You could tell any spanner's story.
My terror of paper's white, tender
but unbounded; period blood; blue
collar. Palimpsest of you,

Father. First frost closed me off, lagging
baa lamb, agèd baby, premature cadaver,
shadow of you, original blue
                              choler worker.

[Sweet almond oil, shea...]

Sweet almond oil, shea, and butter
of roses baste the growing gloom
while evening like a poke bonnet
of blue tulle covers the hill's point.

Still years stood out like a human
flower, a new breed and balance
set the clock in the Time Igloo
whitely to the hour when cuckoos called

and gossip passed from mouth to
mouth with a bite which was slow
on the breeze. And she continued to prey
on her visitors; spray crème de menthe,

with footprints out of green paper and place,
though mine might have fooled her –
she to whom a primrose was always yellow
who dreamed 'from rainbow clouds

there flow not...' Inside, a secret room
is tucked away. Go through growing
gloom – still years continue
and she to dream, to breed, imagine.

[Autumn, most amorous]

Autumn, most amorous of seasons, plumped up
on the divan of the year. Unblinded blue widens
to snap me in. Summer-clothed, yet instinct
with winter, her russet shoulders hug roughly
and her tangerine tongue smoulders
along hedgerows, ripping red through forests
like a zip. Her split skirt, maroon and walnut,
flaps against my skin and cool
slabs, honey-almond flesh, slide behind.

She dangles berries stoked with August sunlight
and pokes them, fattening, through the seams
of her harlequin corset; buckles the stems.

About her flutter saddlebrown smells, muck-rich.
Her eyes know and her tongue tells. I want
to meet her, be sleek by the side of her,
be wrapped in her fulsome pelt, tuned into
her colour therapy. Hush, she comforts,
be rich, feed. Bolt the door against prising fingers
for today. Knowledge and decay. Here the most
beautiful is for now. Here is a perfect pumpkin,
sunny gourd, swollen to its prime:

Autumn splits her bronzing cheeks and laughs.

Now!

said a cheery man with florid cheeks and blues for whites of his eyes. *Turn Now.* And his leotarded assistant, not so young but with stunningly strong brown arms and blue blue ribbons in her hair, sets her shoulder to the wheel, grabs the spindle – turns for all she's worth – till *now* starts churning out in huge gobs and clots, hitting the air like fresh-fried eggs and spinning. She churns *one two three* and it starts coming out at a crazy rate of *nows,* huge potent draughts like oxygen, burning blue skies, glossy leaves on the hedgerow bobbing mad. Bog-cotton hopping. She pushes the spindle skywards, her muscles jumping, and, once it reaches the zenith, it swings round twice with its own weight. Hats and buttoned-up coats go west. People jolt and break off conversations, squint round, curious, to trace the disturbance gulping from a little iron pump in their midst; then look at speaking partners with renewed interest. A wind begins to howl. Married couples forget their vows; row; fall in love. Leotarda turns like a dervish and, soon, pieces of paper, forms, bills, are slapping backwards, and small – then larger – books are being sucked into the vortex. Lanky phone masts waver. Nannies and au pairs gather their charges in the park. A siren sounds and loose-tied, tongue-tied office-workers begin to emerge from shaky buildings, shielding eyes against light and wind. People line the streets, some *lying in* the streets, posing as corpses. Priests who peddled 'deferred gratification' twiddle their thumbs. Boys and girls come to the fore, offering chunks of coconut flesh and brick-red steamed puddings on paper plates. Fruit punch. The air corkscrews, exfoliates, flaying an imperceptible layer of skin till nerves buzz and hum. Fragments of song stream by, long streamers you can snatch, catch 3 at once. The present is here in industrial quantities. Everywhere, moment.

Meddlers

Marplot! Maybe I'll let go of her in verse,
the shrew, her grab-ready hands
and her pinched chin, her volley of quick-
picked cavils, jabbed from needle-tongue.
Sleep-sparing, night-flying daybird,
I'll disembarrass her. Her face
always by mine, hair scraped
back, knitting wool bound
round smallest thoughts. I'll loose her.

Like in a lucid dream
I'll imagine I'm gifted
to rinse myself in citronella,
shake my shoulders, head
for the shore, riverbed tilting
under my feet. I'll write that.
I'll take a breath, whisper 'no' with my will,
coax heart to follow, me spilt and
spelling into blue-white-blue indelible.

Lightning Source UK Ltd.
Milton Keynes UK
UKHW042240020323
417954UK00001B/1